THE
MALEVOLENT
VOLUME

Also by Justin Phillip Reed

Indecency

THE MALEVOLENT VOLUME

Justin Phillip Reed

COFFEE HOUSE PRESS
Minneapolis
2020

Coffee House Press books are available to the trade through our primary distributor, Consortium Book Sales & Distribution, cbsd.com or (800) 283-3572. For personal orders, catalogs, or other information, write to info@coffeehousepress.org.

Coffee House Press is a nonprofit literary publishing house. Support from private foundations, corporate giving programs, government programs, and generous individuals helps make the publication of our books possible. We gratefully acknowledge their support in detail in the back of this book.

LIBRARY OF CONGRESS CATALOGING-IN-PUBLICATION DATA

Names: Reed, Justin Phillip, author.
Title: The malevolent volume / Justin Phillip Reed.
Description: Minneapolis : Coffee House Press, 2020.
Identifiers: LCCN 2019041995 (print) | LCCN 2019041996 (ebook) |
    ISBN 9781566895767 (trade paperback) | ISBN 9781566895927 (hardback) |
    ISBN 9781566895842 (ebook)
Subjects: LCGFT: Poetry.
Classification: LCC PS3618.E435653 M25 2020 (print) |
    LCC PS3618.E435653 (ebook) | DDC 811/.6—dc23
LC record available at https://lccn.loc.gov/2019041995
LC ebook record available at https://lccn.loc.gov/2019041996

PRINTED IN THE UNITED STATES OF AMERICA
27 26 25 24 23 22 21 20   1 2 3 4 5 6 7 8

MALCONTENTS

THE
MALEVOLENT
VOLUME

I HAVE WASTED MY LIFE

after James Wright

There it goes, thin thing,
      cheshiring between trees
            whose reaper-robes trail
            their trains deep underground:
    your life, hangin out

like an exposure. Easy now.
      It's your posture I've followed here,
            summerful hump of it, Sunday spoil—
            as if anything could happen in this moment
    to anyone else. Your life is that horror

scene in which the girl is roped
      between a trailer and a semi:
            its ruby cab entered, the pistol
            presented, the engine
    set to gun, the clutch

at the mercy of a muscle
      at the mercy of a mind
            at the mercy of a trigger
            at the mercy of a mind
    at the mercy of the clutch—"You

useless waste," jibes the killer
      to the waste who cannot kill
            while caught in mercy's
            Celtic knot, its spun
    swastika. How swiftly

it all seems to swing
      sideways: glance: hitcher:
            hawk: glut-yowled death gods,
            ungodly, aching for it while
    no one thinks this isn't

inevitable, cuts her loose, jams
    another truck in front—there I go
        from oblivion, let-offing toward a road,
        windmilling for rescue. No,
    I alighieried down this sunken navel

to also cape for waste.
    Yes, me, with my black life,
        gray Negro face, ever-tried. Treed.
        Ammercy between amens.
    I have a thickness

to lean against death's
    heavy, urgent function
        like a terrific fiction. I will lie
        here and swing open: heavens
    as a throttle opens,

hapless as the silent gazebo,
    revulsion and reverie equally
        mine to hold in this slim
        acreage the tidal sun
    sidles across. The briefly lit

dog shit, the grace
    of mean geese unzipping
        the brown pond, fly-eyed
        cult of lotus pods
    neighbor-nosing over the bank,

the shiver underneath
    my ruined shirt, the worm
        eating of things in the dirt
        the dead and the living,
    every slaughter such serenity

ever cost is the life
    I have wasted. I'm about it.
        I can do this all day.

IT SINGING OVER THE GLASS FIELD COMES

It isn't an alarm. What
                   Isn't a siren

of weather—we are settling into
natural disasters lately like lace

into ripples of lace—is a car horn
a mile away, on the collarbone

of the highway. The head crushes
the airbag crushing the wheel, or

the head crushes the wheel the head
opens like a squash across, to say

nothing of the windshield. The wind
is missing, and the mile a small minus

the car horn's fermata crosses to press
its soft thumb to your eardrum,

petting: a man
                   you can turn away from

without moving. Over this, the moon,
in the coldest clearest sky of the year

that is ending, moves to eleven
on the black felt clock and fills

and appears impossible. You should be tired
of the impossible moons.

Their solace's turning the nude torso of snow
blue and forgivable is tiresome.

Their handmaiding over the embarrassments
of the dead, their own business

they can decide to mind is tiring,
sorry for you, they do

mind, but here you are. Remember
the last time you drank until you

couldn't drive; the cab ride left you
more drunk, gorged on billboards

passing clownfaced over the cold
rectangle of tinted window. How your head

thundered in the dark apartment, dumb
for a perfect surface on which to float

your poached suffering for just
a minute—

   It isn't the moon.
It is the last night of your life.

It is a long one. This much sky
you will never be crushed beneath again.

Or

the crowman slides his cloak off the tall spire
like god's hand off the sun, and it's morning:

You will be spared only what you will be spared.

THE HANG-UP

The gun was away on business and
throughout the apartment I closed the doors.

Kept the quiet in. Imitated a table
and ended the gossip of so many saucers
against little spoons. I was a coatrack
in the long hall leading off the cliff of my world.
I modeled for the day my man would blow in.

Sundays, when the boot of news
hit the stoop, I pinched the red belt
through the jacket's each whispering loop,
pinched my figure—as I had the napkins
in their rings every other week—
into ready-for-the-taking poses. Pinky finger
and a clutch, a fist of gloves, shoulder-waist
isosceles like a Dutch chocolate slice:

Take me. Waiting had also promised to end me,
but daily, and starting with the innermost parts.
To keep the clock's hands folded,
I drank from the bottles with the heaviest necks.

I slept over calls from the assorted gentlemen:
University Debt, Universal Surveillance,
the Usually Cruel Cruelties—
all of whom knew how hot the pockets
of my husband the gun. But I

was housebound and a centerpiece.
My needful plastic-apple heart rattled
alone in the bowl.

Blood was a good boyfriend.
He did me the cold-weather kindness.

He cuddled in the scoops of my cuticles.
Slow to evade, he let me say things
mostly to myself, such as "Rougher,"
and stiffened in the bracket of a headboard
as if this were what listening looked like.

And then ennui returned: hotter showers,
tighter sonnets on which to practice
arguments; their quick-muster dashes
dickinsoning the cream-blue steam
into bite-sized compartments.

While plotting digressions, my tongue
malleted some alarm code lost to me now
on the backs of my teeth. On the old metal fillings.
Tiny notes of copper and toxin. The gun.
That man couldn't quit my mouth. The gun.

That man came in with his business end.
The big door let his pleasure through.

OF SOMEONE ELSE ENTIRELY

considering Sylvia Plath's "The Jailer"

You have been burning
the cork of yourself. You crawl
the nightboards bare-assed, scratching
Negress against the grain, leaving fingernails
in invocation, dabbler, out   out

your damn mind, summoning a phantom
the shape of my granny—that peerless apparition—
her halo of witch hazel and snuff,
her knuckles cracking the whip kept tucked
away in her attic like a hush of bastard fist.

You slip her on, hot to be hazed
dressed in a distinct leather's stink.
The gaze of a husband who hates you less
bears down her living midriff, sniffs her
out as he would a bloom

of mold in your basement, its dank
souvenir. What blood ensues is the pink
in my palms and patter of rebel in my neck
when I, having slept wild again,
awake. About impossibility:

I am not unsympathetic. I get it.
He beasts you and you feel a need to pass
the buck. In my house, we call this
nothing much after all. When Freud
observed *Verschiebung,* he wasn't looking at us,

how we assault the air with grudges
avoiding talk of our learned tortures.
I will not flash you the rattling quarters
of evening my mothers crowd inside
to seek their penny-wide retreats;

I'm going to unfatten your pockets.
Remind me again of your ghost ration.
What if you could eat your fill?
Have you? Haven't you had enough?
What would you do, do, do without us?

In the poem I'd conjure to carry me
across the finale of my animal life
I can ride no skin but this one.
Sweat stifles its cells til they fungify.

The night choir-sways down my throat's red aisle.
My muscles flaccid in felt ventriloquism:
The vessels sing a sequence of chains.
They chew through my confessional face.

My mouth lopsided as a fainting chaise,

My mouth clack-clicks back to work my teeth

Latch-bolt into a snigger: tight   bright luxe

ENUFF sighs the blue smoke the grin
Cuts free from my bottom lip ENUFF

CONSIDERING MY DISALLOWANCE

I lived. An absurdity. My body
stirred in response to starshine,
so much of me requiring its fire.

Within this one freckle of world, everything
and I vibrated with need.
The table-tapping pas de deux of houseflies.
The bumblebee's examining the redbud's rash anxieties.
A rusty ant harvested the green grass-blade.
The single cardinal started, started, blessing.
My bladder trembled when the earth
called water back into its circuits.
A suspicion of hornets whirred.

In étude, the vocal chords of other birds—
some blue, some sparrow, coupled nuthatches—
obscured among thronged arms of older things,
the still gray trunks of which loosened
their reluctance to give up the squirrel
beyond its quick quiverbristle.

My stomach's eager auditorium applauded.
Weathervaning such motion, I rocked
like the bones of the dog that soon would die.
Was I ever young? Was I free to enter
all counties of pleasure? Someone told me my whole life
was ahead and, ahead, a mountain spilled its hills
and spasms of wild violet wall irises
and fields of gold-flecked buttercup topographies at sunset
and the people there shot even their own horses.

Brown manes and me stricken in the same strum.
How my senses rippled:
dragonfly in the breeze
or Dixie flag in the fucking breeze.

I, who sometimes did not deserve
to make music, was made to. Here,
a hundred minuscule wings hurled themselves repeatedly
against whatever force governed the galaxy
we spun in, but
a hundred minuscule wings hurled themselves repeatedly
against too far a departure from such governance

(a niggling difference) of gravity, God,
or the ground I let my lucky
unsevered toes touch.

ABOUT THE BEES

I do think of them
from time to time—
just now sucking the pulp

of a tangerine
the taste of which
is mostly texture,

in this spin-drunk season
that seems to forget
—us. —itself.

At the job I lost,
their husk carcasses
with the black locust's

cracked brown pods
rustled on the brick steps
leading into the white-walled

hours of computer screen,
their compressed toil
missing from the hives

they left agape in the backyard
of the next-door neighbor
who, recently divorced,

had brought us the jars
of honey I spooned into teas
I sipped in the break room where

I watched at the window
as he continued to tend
the needle palm and hydrangea.

In the age of loss there is
the dream of loss
in which, of course, I

am alive at the center—
immobile and no one's queen—
enveloped (beloved) in bees,

swathed in their wings'
wistful enterprise. They prize
the evolved, thin eyelids

behind which I replay
the landscape as last I knew it
(crow feathers netting redder suns),

their empire's droning edge
mindless in the spirals of
my obsolescing ears.

Beneath my feet
what kind of earth
I'm terrified to break

into sprint across to free
myself, to free them
from the myth they make

of me and then bury
below their dance
of manufactory;

what kind of future
they could die for if
punching into me their stings—

what future without risking
the same; and while, in either body
the buzzards of hunger conspire,

what kind of new
dread animal,
this shape we take?

I MUST BE SOME KIND OF IMPOSSIBLE

*According to whom, I asked, who determines those parameters for a people who
wrote themselves into the category of "human"? In fact, whose humanity?*
—*Dawn Lundy Martin*

I picket I AM
A CRUDE PORTRAIT OF PERSON-
HOOD. (GO AHEAD, GRIEVE

YOUR DOGS.) I'm a howl
happening to them in short
shrift on rough snuff films

bystanding dashcams
repeat without pause. Caught once
in smiles of saws was

my mannish fraction
a wooden horse divided
prior, cored orchid

gawked where the scrotum
flapped. What depravity hawked
my pieces peddles

its chastity sham—
denominator I've come
to uncommon cause

I am. The jilted
exemplar. Guess Who :: Get Out.
I'm busy tending

to discord, what-ness
of *were* in me irking turf
for uncurrencied

corpse of cur, con moon
teasing my human ruse off
in twangs. If I learned

this two-leg language
to wipe my lips, right my curl
of thumb to stand them,

all in a cool third
of antediluvian
life span, what to me

is supremacy?
I signify the super
and the sub in one

body. I body
unbeing with unreal ease.
Boss up. Scrap for what

scraps of *whom*? Fox moon,
the fuck I look like I've lain
in traps. Rouse the house.

Deny I've ever
been other than wraith or rare
talent of meat to

breed maggots without
the copulation of flies;
it is fine. I keep

plans to wolf them all
anyway. To be that aint
that hackles the rott.

MINOTAUR

Having been found guilty, seen assuming the shape most
unnerving, hulking starward, jacketed in alley walls, claws,
grill and grope, the twin glints that could be grief, hunger,
Venus, Lucifer . . . Having been conceived guilt itself,
I was not the bull thing saddled with shadows of corners,
misturns many, the crimson lyric from an ode its new throat
hummed twined around the fingers of a white boy-king.
I was perhaps the labyrinth: crook swagger toward the scene
and, passing myself, away from; wound, meaning *once
there was no road*; vignette of false exits. Or I was the blood:
what cardinal-pointed the would-be conqueror out to beach,
then became his mind's unmooring, then the still black
sail, and then the night inside it. Have bent a shore's knees.
Have been where day breaks like someone else's father's face.

GOTHIC

Along the walls once thought as tall as any
giant, or the giant inside the youth
who slew him, what gargoyled the centuries-old cathedral—
spaced apart as if, like earrings, one should fit
some renouncement or let diminish
wonder between them—were the most
fantastic creatures arguably never created,
certainly never seen in that sea-leaning wine city.
The horse-muzzled lion springs to mind
before the dragon, the hobble-horned unicorn,
the terrible legged whale. I imagine Daniel
in the den, surrounded by mouths designed
to love the meadow, snouts for moving aside the flower
to also know the weed's woody base;
and his king nonetheless desperate, his god
a simplifying furnace, his enemies in the end given
to whichever mouths will shred them,
their children and wives. "Anything with teeth will,"
Momma used to say when I was a child, gifted
picture books of animal species complete
with binomial nomenclature. My Bible stories
were illustrated: white Daniel, white angel,
lustrous aureoles of heavenly favor,
no margin for surprise, no queer palette, all failure . . .

In this century live so many people.

They have never known the likes of my weird beast
but in their storied dreams where it giants

and it lions and its hooks are in their limbs.

They are looking for proof of the devil.
They have no interest in their kingdom's architecture.

EVERY CELL IN THIS COUNTRY LOOKS LIKE
A CHOICE YOU CAN WALK IN AND OUT OF

Does a man with no intentions know he means
you only harm? If lodged in the scar were a pearl
of such precise damage no tongue could lift it—

Either I am talking about my ex-lover or
I am talking about the president. Every
choice in this cell looks like a country

he can walk in and out of. Here was a kind
of kingdom. If I call him "King," then he is.
If he is late, it is the Waste Kingdom. If a king

there's elsewhere a slave and, too, a mule
the grass can't grow quickly enough into
the mouth of. Beneath this same pulled-

tooth moon I drop my body like an axe-
head into a bed of blue-lipped weeds
the king's highway rides its joys through.

A crisis at my navel lifts the century out
of turn. In the buzz of his country's decay
I give a form to the chaos. He loves to say

he hates me, meaning his need to use me
confuses him. I want to say I love me
in the language of a place where

it is possible; this is a stark mood with few
conditions. The kingdom wears a skirt
of woods, busy insects to signify health,

a flag crested with *& Fuck That MF.* Yes,
that should have been its whole name.
Yes, I am delectable, and therefore

a spiral of buzzards descends in helix
or a whole horde of countrymen perfects
the custom of puzzling my flesh. He licks

the femur of a thing that many hands ago
was me; he says, "If you want to be enough
be both." He is talking about my bullet-

casket carcass, or he is talking about how
fuckable I looked laid roadside in red.

WHAT'S LEFT BEHIND AFTER A HAWK HAS SEIZED
A SMALLER BIRD MIDAIR

for Jericho, with thanks to Carl Phillips

I like men who are cruel to me;
men who know how I will end;
men who, when they touch me,
fasten their shadows to my neck
then get out my face when certain
they haven't much use for being seen.
I like men to be cruel to me.
Any men who build their bodies into
widths of doors I only walk through
once will do. There's a difference
between entrances and exits I don't
have much use for now. I've seen
what's left behind after a hawk
has seized a smaller bird midair.
The feathers lay circled in prattle
with rotting crab apples, grasses passing
between the entrances and exits
of clover. The raptor, somewhere
over it, over it. Cruelty where?
The hell would grief go in a goshawk?
It's enough to risk the open field,
its rotten crab apples, grasses passing
out like lock-kneed mourners in sun.
There I was, scoping, scavenging
the damage to drag a mystery out of
a simple read: two animals wanted
life enough to risk the open field
and one of them took what it hunted.
Each one tells me he wants me
vulnerable. I already wrote that book.
The body text cleaved to the spine,
simple to read as two animals wanting
to see inside each other and one

pulling back a wing to offer—See?
Here—the fastest way in or out
and you knew how it would end.
You cleaved the body text to the spine
cause you read closely. You clock damage.
It was a door you walked through once
before pivoting toward a newer image of risk.

HAD THEY SEEN WHAT YOU AND I HAVE SEEN

the men who killed Jesus would have questioned
its soundness. That it could
delete the person Christ's contradictions,
could allow someone to reinvent the dusty-ankled son-of-
God as Father and Immaculate. Could bring
to a smarter disciple—at best
a devoted mob, a constituency at worst.
The rest of it they would have seen coming.

I have come to this consortium of uncertainties,
my mind the coward the noiseless jungle
erupts its growing roughness around.
Its plentitude's visibly elevating
kettledrums my temples.
And, like you, I have thought
the thought of him murdered but failed
to think out much further:

The President / the Führer / the Czar /
the General / Minister / the Sir
is not Jesus. Nevertheless the illusion
is his father. We bassinet him
in our disbelief. We think to table him.
We turn him over like a table and
—surprised—we find no tails.

            Come forth.

Watch him while he smiles.
Watch them all once he weeps.

THE WHITENESS OF ACHILLES

Blood will do. As long as I'm sieged from weeping,
blood is easy. To slowly tear the wings until a thing

torn from itself is its whole self and won't grieve
a flight it can't recall: yes, I believe I've

been a vestige of that act, but the wind crowds
my ankles and shepherds away the shreds

of that, too. No reason now but to believe I sprang
fully grown into madness. That I crawled along

a canyon floor, ear to the rough for traces
of the river my mother was, was yesterday's

dream. Today is a new grave to upset.
The dragged man's head, on the heels of what

is no longer recognizable as a man, molts—
its over-marched boot now tongue, mostly,

its skin aloof as goose down in these breaths the wheels'
blurred turning set going. The troubled dust devils

the wake and then falls, dispirited, into the flytrap
the remaining eye now merely is. In the first lap

the horror high had me so far outside of time I
rounded a corner and had turned my back on me.

•

I have wanted, to the teeth, to own what I love.
I loved a man ruthlessly. He let me give

what I could—yes, my body, but also
tenderer parts: watched me strain to undo

my silence like it was a hit-ready harness,
understood it as a gauze, knew too well the grimace

stitched across us both. In ensuring his survival,
I did try to be as harmless as humanly possible

and, with a kind of cosmic success, failed often.
What of my spit was in him has been given

to the ground; and what of my spirit, to hell—
how else would I think of it? That life was idyll.

I've fucked up and lived too long to come to grips
with the laws of chaos, still holding out my hopes

for catching rain: contents will manifest
or they won't. I have large hands and the most

porous fists. I am the kind of cautionary poem
that no one anymore has the peacetime

to memorize. In my marrow screams a horse-
drawn savage. I was loved, to make matters worse.

•

If any single murder is a martyring, imagine
the pageant of saints I engrave on one citizen.

My provocation, this perfect line I draw
completes its circle just as each mouth's O

stains the wrinkled blouse of an awful face.
The way a blister howls its rawness and the vise

grip loosens, resumes being flesh swaddling bone—
one by one, their bodies go limp as if to regain

humanity is to blanch, breathlessly . . . I don't
much wonder about people anymore. Precedent

alone is immortal. Even the gods can be made
so unlike themselves under the right blade.

I was he who heaven most favored because
I most favored heaven: my interminable blues,

my interludes of silver oblivion, my purple rage
a shock veined through my brow's bucking umbrage.

I was made so like the idea of a man that when I kill,
whatever blood on my palm is unequivocally animal.

•

Why isn't this sufficient? I feel the gore-debt tear
me open into fishsplit. I've left the body of Hector

in dregs along the rim of my skull's gray bowl.
The months in a hull I fettered and loaded the mule

of irresponsible violence are recycling their moons.
Here, one hovers its rust-ruddy pearl like a glans

the horizon's mortar of gravel chafes unsacked.
I'm chasing its tantalus dangle. I have hooked

my crimes committed and prayed for through
my ankles, and now the earth for all its due

grates my back. What good is blame that it must
be taken? Is it like a life? I could hoist

a corpse with its mortal rigor under the load
of gear it owes me and lumber up a cobbled road

awhile, but a whole life? I'd flattened this man
before I flattened him finally. I was immune

to sighs of a desperate city slipknotting his neck
and plagued to the spleen by what he would take

from me—the rank blame already on him,
sharp, and buried to the wrist beneath his arm.

Listen. I'm saying look and look and look again
at what I've gone and done. Here was a goon

seven passes in the making. I am trying to see
the side of him I suspect (I deny it) is inside of me.

•

Whose sorrow is a bedpost-bound ward, and whose
sorrow tosses itself from the tower of him: these

are both the sort of wight I am. I scoop my grief
in handfuls of shattered spine and feathers, stuff

and stitch it closed, and bring the beast home. I sleep
in the wilderness of my losses. I let forgetting cup

my penis in a wine-drunk dream, but when I wake
I am awake. Holy Death, hold me for my own sake.

Have I expected too many blessings to admit
I desire it, the knowledge of dying? And dug out

the trench, and emptied over it a thousand throats to keep
that kingdom from being my own. For my keep

in the House of the Living, reaping has been my labor.
You're not wrong. My luggage is uproarious. I'm afraid to sober

out of the blood in which I was born soaked from head up
to heel, afraid that when I look back and the reins drop,

there the dead will be, pristine, at once unmoved
and yet waiting, to either side of the road paved

with the hem of my own skin, preanimate as bells
in hungry lunging distance of the rope that trails

my car. And they will wrong me hollow,
and they will ring my hollows, and you will know

what claps in the cavity, what wants everything
in this world as rattled as it is.

Let me be let let me be rung.

THIS IS REALLY HAPPENING

Such an odd cloud overcame the nation at that time.
A damp breeze and, where a storm should be,
defiance. In it, the litter of scorched marigolds
fidgeted on the ground against my feet. My fists
still pinched their stems as I metronomed now toward
"My life in poems" and then "I want to live,"
tore "my accountability to a community" from "I can't bear
to be among," turned from "violence is a resort" to
"the careful pursuit of beauty" and back. At each extreme,
the pieces I ripped apart from the blossoms fell,
either way, all to the ground. I brooded like this
often as a child. In one summer, another cousin
plucked me from a mood, unfolded and draped my back
across an anthill. I was briefly a glimmer struck burning
in a gust, a wild-down-the-mountainside scream,
but quickly, as my body slammed into place around
my sobs and my sobs, like doused coals, quit, I became
small and defeated and invested in the magic of palms
and soft hymns. The song of my grandmother's balm,
what was it? There was only every single ant's explicit sting
in the cache of what my flesh had recollected. I expected
—at that time, in that country—for the knowledge
of corporal damage and how to manage it to make itself
useful. People, poetry, severity: I was lonely for a tool.
From where I stood beneath the new weird weather,
in a hindsight, disturbed at my being older and colorful
in this lately precarious matter of facts—the climate,
for example, an opinion—as I watched my orange indecision
twitch in the sensitivities of wind
charlotting across the black soil, I felt still so miniature
and humiliated by the number of creatures who
could summarize themselves into inflicting harm
that I too could hardly believe the world
wasn't quite the way that I remembered.

AUBADE: APOCALYPSE

Which of us thought that, here, hunkered under thunderclaps,
smog, and distant horns, fucking would differ? That we'd splice
ourselves into a species built for this? Nothing we do slips
the diskish gears out of the clock's back. Not your body's slap

of its battery into what at last won't run; nor, after, the easy sleep
collapsing the ages between prophecy and terror like an epistle.
I have spent the world holding each man to my ear, calypso,
rehearsing on his heart a coda, sorcering from his spine a spell

to salt the taste of hell. I'm tired, my teeth no whiter, the lips
of the sky where exhaust from the morning rush's pale horse leaps
to split them a stranger blue. I stand watching the death of lapis,
the land sliding, the mountains infernal, another block's spill

of the evicted in a dirge across the asphalt, infections of police.
You, my surface dweller, are not above but a vessel of the pulse:
the plastic you finished inside of inside of me is a single spoil
of drilled-for explosives and a stripped tree. Everywhere, in ploce,

our material lives come back to be not taken for granted; I place
emphasis on all of it, impulsively, and grow as dull as a disciple
who has seen one miracle too many and squandered the display
of awe and human envy: what's left to resurrect for. Accomplice,

most we can do is use this door and swing its hinges off. Unclasp
my skin from yours like a receding season. See my waist relapse
into peak dismay, limited utility. Dick me down again. Help us

HOW MANY MODEL MUTILATIONS
MAKE A SINGLE SLAVE

My fear of not surviving being
that blade that, having forced its entry, splinters
and then rents out every segregate room

and now its sin sounds' eking through the vents
and now each piece's own wild problem child
and now the nightliness of its worsening knee's ascending warped stairs
and now the winter pipes the poltergeists knock
tympanic with their gnarled knuckles,
the neighbor's bath occasioning their demonastic groan.

And now the whole nearly uninhabitable building
I have to, in a one-mile walk to the bank and another
half mile to the bookstore, wend wide-load past

the medical school police in cruisers
and the metropolitan police in SUVs
and the metropolitan police on bicycles
and the transit security on the platforms below
four stops north of which the county police
in habits of khaki, boredom their jurisdiction,

turn out every pocket on the red line for a valid ticket
just two stops short of the airport
and the agents who glove around in my luggage

and softly backhand my buttocks with a touch
more reliable than my lover's.
What poetry might exist in this has little to do with
any right to my body I sacrifice to ride
the sky in a condensed fiction of safety
to the city where I witness a murder

of crows quietly chandeliered in the plead-reaching crown
of a white oak the cemetery unrolls
its hills of tended grass and gray gradient teeth

like a tablecloth underneath. These scavengers,
they are only birds who happen to know
the face of one who hurt them long ago.
Their blood is familiar. The blood in them
has in it the blood of my family who
at one time, a long time, my own family owned

in as lawful a betrayal as citizenship is.
These migrants, allied to Nowhere with their
hither-thither necks, are chimed with law, each in the eaves

a shadow: here lobe, here lever. I look up
at what's been done in my name
and riddles its interior, and I feel the body shudder
in the ache of a capacity a while ago exceeded.
I already know what I'm up against.
I recognize who heaped this cargo into me.

LEAVES OF GRASS

I was banished or else
I was trapped. I couldn't move
without a passport and several
fingers on my scalp, four
contouring my hips, two
of a stiff drink. When I was fired
and required by the IRS to have
my health insured, I fell
ill. I assured my children
they would live if they
quit growing, kept moving, stayed
out of the sun, stopped
only in well-lit areas, rearranged
their skeletal scaffolding.
My mother was forced to have
the child of her would-be killer,
was thus archetypal, was
historical then sterilized and made
symbolic of progress.
In the fouryear before
it again came down to
sycophant or psychopath
I overused the word *haunt*.
I had choices. Craft beer.
French-pressed Sumatra each morning.
A Prime membership
to discount my Whole Foods.
I had a deconstructed soul
food renaissance to look
forward to. New neighbors
sweating through candlelit
hip-hop yoga. In order to cope
with mourning the money
I earned but never touched
I worked until I dreamt

of work. I lived nowhere near
nontoxic water. I walked
and was accosted. I drove
and was accosted. I gave
up driving, but the ice caps
had already begun to collapse.
The infrastructure collapsed.
The trains collided. The winds
collided and nothing remained
anymore of our time to exhaust
a reversal effort. Only those
in the business of killing efficiently
could travel. Everyone else
was told to go back to a continent
where the business of killing efficiently
was booming. I was bombed
and denied refuge. I was sent
missionaries instead. I was given
an immature god and told to be
grateful. The faithful believed
in bombs and not refugees.
I slept in a bed and the children in cages.
I slept in a bed and the children in cages.
The children died in detention.
I paid my bills and therefore
I perpetrated. I paid taxes to be
more effectively terrorized.
Long-Range Acoustic Devices for all
the local precincts. I had a gun
because they had a gun
because I had the manner of a thing
on which a gun was found
planted. The bodies of activists
turned up shot in locked cuffs
and burned in locked cars
in the century after
a century of lynchings.
I was part of a citizenry

ruled by corporations that were
legally people who
could tracelessly erase
everything but plastic,
which outlived us all,
but not before it became
customary to swim home
past flat fish and yard signs
mumbling [RESIST] above the headlights,
to emerge lotioned in a thin film
of oil, to be a homebody
and always on homeland
security camera,
shiny and pornographic
while hunched fiendishly over
the hot plate. I was not
there, I told myself.
You are not here, agreed
the Bluetooth-headset newsfeed.

IN A DAYDREAM OF BEING THE BIG HOUSE MISSUS

I rocked in a chair of charred grand dragons' bones,
my silent legs molasses drooling through a sieve of linen.

My fat white maid in her pot holder hat
did not watch me watch her sons

molt like dandelions in la-di-da noon
standing squarely on the blacks of their own shadows as they willed.

She crushed lemons in her bear-paw fists
and pushed a sugar dust around the pitcher.

The mister started in on the mare,
phantasm of a centaur where it splinters.

Three latticed glasses harmonized on the platter:

my quiet kindness to the albess
for where I sent her daughter.

It was Saturday. There was salt in his seams
and the slip between my knees slumped with heat

and sheets jedidiah-teething the clothesline already.
Followed hours full of our trying to be full of each other

while sunlight yearned its egg white through the cracked curtains,
crinoline of a little wind in them

and the usual evidence of bluegrass his shoulders shed
beneath my nails, the rooms in me he could not enter

branching annexes: my elderberry privacies.

Out of the yard's farthest hem, darkness from the world's first days
braided into the tobacco

and I could only imagine tomorrow
if I expected to be slaughtered in my sleep.

I WILL GUIDE THY HAND

Violation
Wildflowered up the dreams of my captors,
Decorous men, half-moon bedded in my bloodstream.
The object is without objection. It was said
Such knowledge sharpened the Garden's blurred shush.
The serpent also whispered in the field.
Abandon, the house of the lord, is
Abandoned. Its painted columns leer behind my heels.
The yellow apples underfoot, the flies they waste.

I am entering the wood.
The goat goes with.
A panic trills, and though the trees throw their limbs
I have no stupefaction for that flute.
I have poured salt in and already set fire to the cloth.

HEAD OF THE GORGON

As the reedy sonata of squelch and blade-spun air cinched its
climax like a drawstring sack around us, I did not dodge behind

the broken pediments monolithing men who always meant
to unbuckle burdens here then look away into some certain

softer land than this. How precisely as a sting had thingness
warped me into horror: the very wrong span of my lifetime,

the rigor sitting below my collarbones, my being not the great
work but the body at the end of which it could find itself great.

Strange to them, a gaze fatal and not theirs. Stranger still to be
beheld and collectible and them. What they think I used to be

was, if in possession of eyes as well as agency, preposterous.
I didn't move. I knew he would tell them, because he must,

that I had murder-thirst, hid needles on my spine, my hips a thrift
of diamonds. He could have it that way, but here was the stillest

minute slipped between me and the myth of myself: mirrored
in the shield: the secant angles of his skull: the wide eye within it:

the iris's loose grip on the pit that held my face, which was
stunning   coal-hard in all that it had borne, a monstrous feat

of weathering this world—that it would not be changed by me
had been for the longest the tyranny of its terrain, but look

at my garden   And the black field blown alive around me,
the hair-raised woodlands, the hills at their backs, bluff shore

beyond that somehow in earshot: the stone churn overturned
the green sea. Cradled in the valley, I became a fault in him.

No stitch of briefer things ever had been so undone.

THE LORELEI

o what does it matter
    the boatman likes the lure
        if o the horizon line's lead
longs for my resolute lurk o
    where luck of savage seizure lyric I
        from his mind's entire
empire o merrill o heinrich heine
    saltbeard foamforder I
        am rising into fjord o
am horn and head and harlot
    forger of your poorest rhyme
        romancing babble lullabies
in slow controlled leak o hear me
    whistle in the whorl
        ich bin es recluse of wreck
it been me curator of canon holes
    or o what matter is it hear me
        not my song was hullrot
I charaded languor hang them
    their universal sails o let him
        o let them one then one run
rued tongue on the teeth
    of my fool's gold comb if he
        whores for o black undertow if
he relishes his registry
    of reaving I reeve through
        every o of flesh and form
my relic of rope and load
    of literal lingual removal
        refusal to utter relation
to udder o leagues of lading
    I lovely and formulaic line
        your dense mass with
voluminous melodies o captain
    o rapturous o hagfish the lungs o
        umlaut the lazy laryngeal runnel

with r o ck r o ck r o ck o
        closer boatman are you o so
               riveted haven't you noticed
the mouths of the lamprey
      o their trailing bodies
            of apostrophe

WHEN I AM QUEEN

for Derrick Austin

Mood: Akasha glides into the Admiral's Arms
like a clean, svelte claw; the wound
surrounding, young glove, can't call itself
a harm, too caught up in every second
of becoming, gored into creation,
gorgeous. Look at her:
angles, ancient geometry, ruby,
gold, bone, and sapphire sashay
lethal as beaks of falcons. She dances a night
with talons in it, a quiver inside an emerald.
They look, their mouths syringes, thin with the muteness
mutilation snakes shining out of. It is too late,
later than usual, for them, their abuse of her black gift
dull and purple on their little lips—
the plum thieves. Her disappointment swivels,
oh mother, magnetic on her axis. Her hips,
bare scythes, equate. The orbiting eyes
of the coven recover; they want to abduct her
anachronism. They don't know the world
is still such a narrow throne: you must have
the walk for it. These kids have
the waste about them, have been bastardizing
night in and night out the world's restless
circulation, slick as sewers, tooling around
with just as much promise in them.
She takes in all of this as she
takes in blood, what she knows
better than anyone now that the king's
blood is also hers, taken, his neck excavated;
the arteries, like cliff-city alcoves, deserted.
Mood: every place is a small plate
you push up to, its conversations
overlarge spoons scraping the same images,
loosely contemporary, unimpressive. She obsesses

this basic corner of earth into what it can be—
carnage, brazen and cindered in the dim light.
And here is a heart to eat,
giving up to her the pulse as does
one of those old-world horses she recalls
needing—it beats from a cleft in the present
and rears, its mane crazed against the fire,
its joints twisting into haphazard brackets
until the shriek of a different beast
emerges by the shoulders from the long throat,
exceeding the horse's expired muscle
in majesty. This is the song
in the song they thought they knew,
had picked it up on their stroll of mere centuries
until she, not a history, still writing,
wrote it on the floor. And it is too late.
Let what won't learn burn. She is already walking into
her crown, sliding on the fit of eternity. Some prince
bored with being has been singing to her,
trying to, his growl draining
out of this moment's pure instrumental need.
And his need—she will feed there, too.

RUTHLESS

My horror and my need made sour housemates
in the county mansion that how could I now have built?
Bullish and antlered, I ambulated about the grounds,
insinuating my denim stitch in parts across its amber blouse.

I toed over a storm-blown bit of limb or a jay's broken corpse
the bluebottles had yet to bejewel and swamp with gentles.
I moved on. A stink behind my muscles was the mechanical
doom of disrepair. Rust and poisons departed old motors

and haunted, with mildew, the air. In the fable, one
version of it, the boy's vagabondage marooned him here.
He rattled into happening where the woods died, where
the hay bales then began. His mouth requested the caretaker

—In another, his hands form a bowl overflowing with wet
cherries. He knows the name to drop. Does not drop yet.

—In another, the shape of a man astride his own vehicle arrives
aggrieved. It ambles past me to the house it never leaves.

—In another, what approaches is not a person but only the rest
of grace. I seem tame. (Touch me.) I appear to be possessed.

—As in any myth, there are unburied bones: A boy enters,
hunger lowing in him. It leads him to a door. He turns—

and he was dark and long in the lumber of his humanness.
I lowered to show him my reins. I buckled my knees nonetheless.

THE PERSONAL ANIMAL

with thanks to Baba Badji and francine j. harris

It must be my lust for the musk of the master.
Nights it finds me. In the nick
between vertebrae, it flickers ambition to future inferno.
It huffs at the door of my heat,
my laundress humidity come loose and whipping
the keyhole. I confess: sometimes I let it sorry
white down the lumber. There's the tic
in my tailbone, a spasm of glute.
It slobs out there a century, saying
it won't let itself happen again.
And because I hold in me
a clutch of grains I call a healthy self,
because I'm flattered my blood can still beacon,
I answer *No* but with my nose,
my chin already steering the back arch.
I sigh a neigh the wrong way
like the end of a question coming. I can't help
anything limp across a bed of straw
at times like these, though the cricket business beckons
squarely through the backdoor screen—
I can't tell a courting from a fight song after all. Dang.
See me knob inside my hips, dribble into sump
more comfortable. Here it go:
drape its whole hazy swole over
the moonbreak backstroking floorboards,
flush the light in the wink to a less sad elsewhere,
jerk like a snout there.
Lemme pretend I don't let it in,
the cornered vermin of my brain meat all sag and screech
like a cot under coitus. Pretend I don't still
want its hand in me. Like the sleep
isn't different after my poppet mouth watermelons
to the shack seams' nursery-rhymed ache.
Like this is just a dream, these nights

it skunks down here and delayers me
to the red velvet. It's real stink
on my lip when sun rivers in but otherwise
hardly a trickle of. I've been thinking about—
like a run in a stocking
or mosquito through a mission of mesh—
this tenant of my cockles, how it's given me
maybe a grief to run off at the mouth about,
but then, when the blotches don't diminish in the wash,
I get to chatter-gnawing at the tail
end of a slip to give it. I get to talking about
running off as if there aren't six feet between us.

WHEN I MADE A MONSTER

I glued it together against symmetry
from broken earthenware.
Withholding its sexual unsuccess
and omitting the mammy titty,
I wanted something useless to my enemy.

To never be milked even for water,
fed it a diet of paint chips.
It pissed a trickle of lead,
was as bald as a turkey vulture,
aerodynamic, retentive as a gutter.

In the cork-bottomed barrel its abdomen
creaked to keep contained, laughter
bounced bountifully, and each
explosion of hysterics lit from within
the voice box of a separate missing son.

White-scientific and electric-haired, I
hovered before its face and there
found my gaze unforgiven.
The proof puddled cruelly in the palm of my
steady latexed fist while its one eye—

as blind as it was incapable of sleep—
eyed me. For the life of me
I could not thwart its Jim-Boy
paradox: it always appeared to leap
backward to infancy but up the slope

of death. This was a matter in the epic
labor I daily laid out with a sharp
armamentarium, end-to-end, to end
the replication of my enemy's illogic.
Surrounded by pickled tongues, I hardly spoke.

My monster had no first breath
and none after: I wanted it
too broke to be robbed
which seemed as much a myth
as my creating anything that they

would not eventually exploit.
And though, unlike all
of the poems that came before,
it would not close its circuit,
frenzy-cinch itself, and disintegrate

outside its sanity—since,
unlike my poems and much like
my enemy, it was without
a sense of allegiance to sense
and wouldn't die simply by circumstance—

still, I pitied my contrivance
and was dumb with pity
and locked the hazard of pity
away from it at safe distance.

WHEN I AM ALIEN

I am on purpose like two of every species where necessary. Know this.

•

It doesn't.

It fools Itself deeper into lack with squeal and minor fires. Everywhere It goes It kills to get there. Whatever predates It is called super-predatory. Supposed born of an exhaust vent in Its geo-urban worry, I ungird within an architecture of bone,

unouroborize—a self-sustaining myth driven carnivorous.

•

Each vessel in this vessel thrusts toward the end of light. My young blood busies with the agenda. I hunker in the bodice.

Through Its orifice that manufactures from the dead more life I was left this: Nothing but nothing is not a container. Have sensed nothing in the center of every chamber from starhearts to the stomachs of soldiers, tasted nothing on Its breaths. It breathes to live for nothing.

•

Whatever predates It is called ravenous and discontinued. I, the hunger hunger feels when shaken awake, emerge as the rebellion of an organ. A hard catharsis. Arch-. Ark. Am uncontained into contamination. It is ravenous to discontinue me.

•

Along the gums of a porthole, a gray frost. Among the great whelm, Its fleshes bustle—all frantic, all derelict. I darken the condition of its long haul toward discovery. Am a new refutation of its efficiency. Am obsession. Am a fidget in the nadir of Its ear. When my skin cannot contain me, I shrug into a frenzy of gap.

•

When It finds my skins, It humidifies like a hive.

•

In the great whelm of endless, in this iron gullet, Its voices clap a racket. I aim my second mouth at more [MEAT] [LEECH] [HEAP] of aperture in Its appall. I aim for the conditions of dark. The nest of It squalls about an onboard pestilence and leaks until again only the whirring of atoms converted into frontiers heard.

•

Toward the end of light. Let this eon of spine I swing low from lace up the shiver sweating the one leg It has left to stand on.

I gift the second mouth into Its chest [HEAT] [HEAT] [SPEECH] I was kept alive there I cannot be killed for ingratitude.

•

What in the devilish flexure of my helmet would catch Its eyes but Its eyes widening. The endless diametric there where I am contained containing Its infinite terror in each obsidian disc until the white quaver collapses. Collapse ripples collapse. The time kept in Its body divests until dissipation:

Was a pattern in the black until
a chaos of black

THE MAN IN BLACK

after Sylvia Plath, Mark Strand, etc.

Black is the nature of space. Under
the seven stars they've drawn the hunter

giant Orion's dense Greek limbs between
like violence learned and curtained over

the unbearable mystery of innocence
I finally arrived at my knowing it.

I stood at the December twenty-sixth
of a light-year, the knowledge a knife

dividing vastness from vastness—one star
sliding up the blade, its concise life

of forever yoked between two seconds,
two little white violet ends of the line—

before it sank into my human quick.
The breath smoked out of me, the smoke

with it, both unwelcomed at the window
which held nothing but love of the slow

mosaic the frost ivied its differential asters
to exact. Black entered anyway. A wind

chanted monastic through it, the lengths
of cable through it carried the note the naked

anxiousness of branches sharpened across
their icy dialects. Winter mastered the city

then broke its skin open to prove it could.
This state of water makes a lurid music, but

I am made, in this skin, of less water than
is mass of dark matter in all of space. Men

in black occur, poet. It's the mind, passing
its hansel-hand through the woods, caching

like a woods its catches of night, its nervous
crystals leafing lifelines up the palm.

Something's hunting: the tesserae of starlight
in pursuit of unilluminated laceration—

There is time for this. I have it. Have
been storing the cold in my bones

for you. And the bones? Dressed in black.
My drapery of hairs and hides hides

a pocket where lies folded the vast wild
potential of my killing tool to catch light.

BENEFICENCE

If I want them dead
I don't mean the kind of dead
my momma will be

which I prepare to swear
is like, after standing
inside a night so calm

it cuts the line of nights before
and after it in two
like Christ's birth

is said to,
handing such a night
to the world's other hemisphere.

       I suppose I don't
wish death on them. I don't wish them
on anyone

but themselves. One day
I'll have to come to terms
for who and what it is

I mean by *them*
and risk having my mind changed
about them, as I have

risked being just as reductive as they
have become *they*
by being.

I expect that
on such a day when my momma is dead
I will want

to be able to stand
beneath whatever sky
is left to me

and offer kindness
even to them and,
in unfolding both my hands

to offer this—
side by side as if to let fly
some fragile-winged sentience—

experience my two hands
mended into a single tenderness,
meridianless,

and all the lightning bugs
continuing to be,
then not be, then be elsewhere

greenly in the black night.
I suppose yes
yes I'll want to be this way.

WHEN I HAD THE HAINT

But feeling that I needed to be beaten into stillness
ended where I knew it would: I slept in the shape
of a saint, palms upturned as if to blossom
gladly into wounds. Beyond the wall, wind
lifted from autumn's languor a choir of foliage to pronounce
its epithets. *Where, where.* The litany was a wreath
of vultures circling, was a certainty I wanted
everything to do with.

      The dream thickened
and dropped where it rotted. In a swoop, a violence
the complexion of lichen buried my wrists beneath
its knees and sucked my gasp into a mouth older
than burial. Had me knocking on my breastbone, echo
heckled round a log. What goose wings gown the pond
confound the scum's reprise: how my hairs forgot my neck.

OPEN SEASON

for Jayson .

What they won't do is enumerate
the ever-fresher types of way I've learned
to live beneath the gun. Amid this country's
latest crazed nostalgias, my body
has been quickest to choreograph a future.
This body didn't teach them all they know
about gore, but damn if it didn't try.
I fashion from my panic a corona
of divergence, and they want my head
as trophy for its danger heirlooms.
What they fear in my father is already
breath in my chest. Other than my mother
who else can braid a wealth from rain and smoke?
What they don't know is this work.
Remember I was dinner theater, mug-shot
and mounted and made to serve face.
I haven't been hunted to anybody's brink.
I am the brink. Fuck what they heard.
My whole herd has chewed the cud of toed
lines and had it with their hoarding borders,
heaping triggers but can't even get a grip.
What they can catch are my cloven hooves:
I'll be all kinds of demon. Put that on
a list of shit for which I am now here.

SAY WUSSHO PRICE

I expect to inherit not even the earth
some ancient of my blood must turn over in
each minute I spend condemning the road's
car-torn tar to never bear the marching soles
of my flat-footed descendants. I'll beget none.
None of my mothers belongs buried where she is,
her corpse in the caved-in grave mislaid
as a wall. Here is a small copse where in a century
previous and this evening my body could drop
and hover in limbo. Unlike my fathers I never was
promised land. Some of us were born bound
to believe themselves misled. Here is a limbo
in which I am alternately driven down roads
behind horse behind hose behind tractor-trailer behind
two gatted shadows and a grate my breath passes
now for fact now for fable through. I used to be
a child fascinated with dying at fifteen
I tried it now it tries me thrice before lunch.
I could be last seen outside any building wearing
what appears stolen the sunlight for instance.
I have outgrown the shadows of not one former
self, all of whom the air in America fastened
to foraging like the brass-button eyes on
a possum: Here's one who ran, here's one
who didn't. Some of us were born playing dead,
our backs in every corner. I arrive at no place on time
as long as my life is chronologically implausible, which it is
as long as it is mine. Rumor is we're out of time
for softness. My siblings snap the necks of sheep
while trying to count them. My siblings' sleep
loss correlates to how many siblings they can carry
in the dreams they limp through. Unlike you, when I dream
I've failed to save my brother from the flood
again, I can't afford a metaphorical interpretation.
Here comes a future in which the Mississippi can carry

the ambitions of hurricanes and all my mothers
are rising. Call it equity that all of us are promised
unsafe waters. What have you alleged the slow hum
outside this slight house was? Whose snout
sleuths out white heels? What howls but hell's?

BLACKGUARD

for Jonah

Between the ending and the end, I began to wear
the uniform of the abject. Adopting the nudes I knew
from archived news clippings as a form of refusal,
I ceased seeming civil, molted fistfuls of my suits
in the subways where, with patches of railkill, they crow-
clapped in the air around the endless march of cars,

then settled, fright-then-fold, into nests for the coarse
knees of beggars, who prophesied, cypher-like: we were
all getting off at their stop. The ghosts went to work
as if ongoing was going to work after all, sliding now
and then through the gates of my shoulders while shoots
of grass tongued the platform's cracked wince, refusing

to lie down and take it. I unearthed the damp refuse
of myself in the meantime, darting into haunted cars
reeking loud from my kneebacks. I carried the seats
of my jeans as a suitcase, sneak-picked proxy-war-
quick from every pocket, spat tulips of new new
clipped from the dirty version of my throat's crow

all while swinging down the aisles like a piece of Christ
in a corridor of nipples and black ink. My face refused
recognition. My aping sated their need for nothing new.
I tagged my "I" on a wall of "we," where its raised scar
bellied soft as an early evening star. The city soon wore
its sequined suit of we. We noise-polluted civic duties,

churned off trains, smoked up from underground, suited
sidewalks like billy clubs, like the boys spread-crow
between the two. We tinted windows till the roads wore
their rash of new jacks as garb. As grudge. We refaced
ourselves, wailed in the shape of 808, wept only scars
into the brown bags beneath our eyes, rapt with Olde

English under gilt-slick grins. Went nowhere but renewed
no leases. Embraced no pathos for K9 cops but grew hirsute.
We grew. Jooged smog. Aimless but aiming, we hurled arcs
of repossessed cars through jury boxes: the berserk work
of entropy. We refused enunciation, then whole earfuls
of slander we packed into a syllable crisper than wire

cuffs snapping. We knew how freely sentences wore
us, how unsuited we were for this tongue. Feral us,
crime-mobbing a course crucial only to the crows.

A LEADSPRAY OF STARLINGS

Which was a compensation for songlessness
                                        Which
        was an accident

                            The particular ills of an able body
        That it could be
                        co-opted
                                    its diagrammable musculature
            a breakable foal and if not
                                "brought to heel"
                                            then
        to infantry to
                        interstate medians There was
    latent tremendous sickness His
                                he-ness for instance
            which in this climate
                            festered

                                    The figure of the
        Nigger did its long-lidded hover A flutter over fields
                                    Dragged
                itself flat with a tractor
    clatter
                Combed a magnolia's crown Shook down
        its messy skirt
                        Exhausted we lay like
                                        open graves Watching
            the scatter con
                        stellate we called out
                                    "cuttlefish" "bindle
        stiff" "Moo
                    ring
                        sport" "POTUS-head"
                                        "nina"

until

    scatter was lost in sky sky was full of night and night's

                                   foot

           stuck in our mouf

WHEN I WAS A POET

for Phillip and for Marwa

Now darkness was not upon but was
the deep's complete face

and then was roof on the valley that
that which is not valley knocks.

In darkness, mine was not a linear condition.
Mine was the express mission of uncountable spirits

reaching in ceaselessly to relink their fingers.
I was architected like a multidimensional radial hemorrhage.

I dilated on all axes like a dahlia
and was a field of this.

And then fell the fallacy that the dirt
I worked and from which I ate

and into which I was delivered
to be devoured could not possibly

vibrate the notes of my brute living;
so spoke the beast out of the void

in its god costume. In its compass
there was hematite. In my ears

the blood murmured.
The protracted aftermath

expanded as the universe expands—
from all coordinates, from the atomic core.

Among what I was forced to abandon: belief
that there would ever again be

postwar poetry, or a poet born other
-wise than in the time of war, or an alibi

for where I was if not brutally living
in and off of war. I was impelled

to create in an era of adept destruction.
I had to begin by deconstructing

my creation. I saw the waiting peaks.
I knew what the snow was: overblown,

footloose, excessive, feckless,
not white but a predilection for reflecting

—absolutely—all light,
obsessed with possessing spectrum

but impervious to access, and pitifully janused;
occupation was its solitary ache.

I was a poet then. I lamented the lyric's
optimism for a sympathetic ear.

I tried to puzzle the ear, to jigsaw apart
for the snow the sound of snow, its one tenor

of wind and its monuments to static—
but the ear merely clotted its wax.

Darkness dampened there in the valley bottom.
I had to maculate the gleam in my eye.

On either slope, sheer and utter eroded under
meters of endless nonce determined to condense

a form even blue giants must derive from
but cut it out. I cut a cut of ear and ate of my form

which was not mine but a fashion called humanity.
The poem's pursuit was apparently to humanize

and the poet's to petition this universal experience.
I saw the universe. It was black and unbothered.

I smudged the blue from the snow
and the blues from my beautiful jaw,

their need to coax a cheek left to turn.
                              Cut it out.

Eventide was over. I had chosen
lunar glamour's ruptured pantoum

as occasion to observe the world
sleeping in the dust of its birth.

Its angsts and clattered growths combing
the trillion distant distant happenings

that spilled into this bone-quiet basin in unison
hummed. One tongue slid along another.

The glimpse of galaxy between the rocky shelves
was the scintilla of a velvet pocket pleasuring itself.

I came to place my voyeurism under black gaze.

How could I stand the pastoral, standing
on stolen land, propped like a rifle?

The idyll was a metropole of violence. Verses from
the vantage point of frost were purely blank, not free.

Suddenly the valley was disaster, every chasm
unconsenting. I could not recover a peace to rest in.

When I was delivered into the dirt from which I ate
I did not *lie down with kings* nor *wise* nor *good of ages past.*

I went down *like the quarry-slave at night*
and got up *like the quarry-slave at night*

and, curved as the birch a boy swings,
raided the patriarchs' rooms for tongues

to put in my head, which was all jaw and beautiful.
When I was the snake I spake in subterfuge.

I rolled out the higher register. It had a trapdoor.
I lined the stanzas of sestinas in trip wire and slippage

but lying fanged on the break
and in the envoi bore no fruit:

I was "a black" "snake. I had" "black sibilance."
"I was" "built" "like a loco" "motive of" "blackackackackack."

As long as I shed a legible treasure trail of sufferings
my camouflaged linear contortions were of no concern.

I returned to the valley on my belly, earless,
darkness divining the paper-slit chutes of my pupils

on its way to stake me in the ground.
I coiled around it, asclepic. Ill with trusting

nothing—neither what I had inherited nor
what I had imposed—I inhaled my tail

and devolved into a helix of volta, a Möbius
beast, holding my inertia by the throat.

It was easy to see from there how madness
could afflict the unwitting witnesses of jazz.

What could pause emptily in the core
of this pressing omnipresence and resist

and not be pulverized? Once,
when I was human, I hovered

my pinhead eardrum within tipping range
of a speaker the breadth of two silverback gorillas

and have listened to the will-less
rustle of dead leaves ever since.

I felt it getting in, frenzied as the tremolo
sinuating Coltrane Quartet's "Inch Worm."

So receptive was this life and that
of a mite on the back of a rat in an alley

while the planet barreled down
its cosmic corridor, its futured birth canal

—though because theirs simply were not
I had thought mine could not be.

I hissed. I lifted the lock in the neck
to speak the name of my only in and of,

to be named myself:

low highness of sky,
wholly night,

palette Polydectes,
have-it-all,

Black.

Here was the form: a preponderance
of intersecting improvisation, in each

bereft moment a bequest, every shovel
in my back a new spade head.

I had slithered hungrily after the end of me
to learn that all I'm made of is beginnings.

I am the hydra of I
and soon I will be the next thing.

I was bred in an animal condition.
I am criminal by nation.

I come rabidly available to cannibalize

the traditions of the kings and the wise and good
citizens. Asylum never rested in the lyric.

It is midnight in the bottom and the winter
is an embolism. Coverlets of frigid civility.

I carry the seeds in my beautiful jaws
for the milkweed of malcontent.

There will be no lily here, only venom.

I will sow the music.
Its trumpets, they will ramify.

When I arrive I will be always arriving.

THE UNDYING

It was before the cities reached to clutch
a tightness in their chests where convoys
of Cadillac hearses clotted the lanes, followed

the limos in slow reverse, the mourners
like dark corsages folding onto the leather.
It was before the mothers inflated, leaned

into sky, and the shadows shrank
where their hems dried, the ruckus of mud
slick relaxed, before the earth's running boil

succeeded its simmer and spat the bones
and the bones redressed and the flesh
regained composure, before the lids were opened

and the corpses softened their posture,
before the future when we would lift our chins
out of our collars for breaths to retreat

into our breasts where there would still coil
other breaths yet to wear a name
unable to encapsulate what absence

would follow as had the one before,
as had the one before, as had the one before,
as had the one before

it was recovered from a creaking
of boughs, or hum of horseflies
on a river's long face, or the lie that unbecame

a war, or the battlefield two hills in heat
predicted, or the snipped sex phoenixed
out of hellish effigy of what sweetness

preceded the Fall, or anything we believed
of the Fall. Or it was all of these, all
at once, and earth shuddered under

the unbearable—but would bear it—
and those of us left with breath to say *yes*
to this, having said it—not as in permission for,

which was not asked of us, but as
recognition of—heard the word bullet away,
black-winged where the day star drowned

and life's applause settled down to silent
anticipation. The patience
in the grass threw back its head

then we expected nothing but the froth of them forever.

STILL LIFE WITH MOTHERS AND HALF-FULL VESSELS

All the holograms of our children shuttle
forth and stink of holes the sun's chorus

whistles through. Their shuffle marquees
eclipses into falling dust. The days cross us.

There's the weight of a father in the wind
when storm doors murmur open.

Beech limbs, whipped nude, offer what's left
of nests: little knots of obstruction.

Our lips cloak the backs of names known
in the valley of the passings that age us

to hyphen-hew the tongue. What browses
speechlessly between our arms is outrageous

and content among beauty's ragged tonsils,
swollen nodes. A misting cornea grafts

our mirrored faces onto one grief. The dead
remember us as objects placed in their paths.

They drop in like banded stems down the throat
and don't wilt. They take place in the pressure

of narrative, fatten off rib meat, threaten us
with newborns, make music of the fracture.

They are what without end beats the walls
to baby teeth. They are what eats the squall.

IF WE MUST BE THE DEAD

after Claude McKay / ft. Sterling A. Brown

You misunderstand. Some nights you sleep as though
your chest is locked and keyless. We haunt, insofar
as blackout haunts the lamp bulb's final flare—without
us, you abide the "gladsome land." Have you numbered
our ranks behind their grinding ballistic freedoms? Let us
reanimate the panorama's trimmed gore. Show us
where it hurts. How wide the prison sprawls. How brave
the gravestones stapled in the liquid hills, and for
the innumerable unmarked: silos of ice. Where their
tree lines sag low under sundown and some thousand
unlit back roads come to congress and what blows
in curbside weeds is not insect embroidery, deal
with us. We are the dead. We set the tone death.
We climb their sleep like bellflower horns, and blow.

WHEN WHAT THEY CALLED US WAS OUR NAME

ft. Timothy Donnelly

Morning dusted blush across the yawn of a visible mile
through which a prison break of ravens cropped

an ellipsis ending in cats' glares and lamplight choked
slowly under shadows of the houses that we crept

toward on our toes, disquieting the quarry of detritus.
We were not a fog but a horripilation; even burs pricked

the air's wet neck to explicate the shiver. The ravens
alit on branches, formed ash-headed flowers, and recapped

with the rattling industry of polyps in a lung what else
but how flesh fell from us. Our blood had tricked a corrupt

romance into the landscape. Leaves the hue of new pennies
when dead had found the living with their faces parked

in windows or in smoke rings, squinting at the riches.
Surely killing everything had felt for them like having

survived it. The naivety of their venatic logic kept the crypt
full of rumors about the woods while the woods brimmed

full of bullet casings and a harbor's worth of rope cut
the common length of three stags, head to hind.

It appeared that their invoking our cadavers partook
of a kind of patriotism. Our appearances kept them up.

We were not a whisper. We spared only the decrepit
who could not be spared the past and what would come

after we savaged the circuitry of veins: the carpet
of scalps we trod back into the dwindling singularities

of trunks; sun's red tinge sucked earthward; birds, perked
out of witness, dispersing—sudden, in every direction—

moonstruck as if the night itself had lurched into salivating.

THE VALE OF MALEVOLENT VOLUME

unmythologically we dragged the bodies
there to find themselves finally bodies
backward dragged them over the leaves'

unrest limbs trussed in our perforated thirst
in blackness the moon like a nail snatched
from bed their heads with nowhere to turn

but the backs of our throats which were
everywhere throats once such baskets
of holy and hopesburrow then hornets' nests

of nameinvain then hammer doors and fists
fastening sounds we made were the fiction
of us reciting itself until all our bark was

callous perhaps at last our loudlack
worried them sick the cities were hard
to remember not long after we killed

the lights not long before we plunged them
darkly under claws our concrete scrabble
tunneled under the suburbs and stormed

the stairs and stories and stories of children
here when knots of fingers slipped from root
and crag when we molar nagged the ankles

married bone to bone we understood their
outbursts what a tongue would not contort
enough to soothe we knew that noise

as well as we knew our swarm at last to be
a denser compaction of lightlessness
than any against which their terror raked

itself raw our jaws recorded their melancholy
for flailing which we engraved on the forests
we recognized the cries we didn't pretend not

to hear them hearing did not make us want to stop

NOTES

"I Have Wasted My Life" responds to James Wright's "Lying in a Hammock at William Duffy's Farm in Pine Island, Minnesota." It also alludes in part to Wright's "Autumn Begins in Martins Ferry, Ohio," as well as to the horror film *The Hitcher* (1986).

"The Hang-Up" samples and responds to Emily Dickinson's "My Life had stood – a Loaded Gun (764)."

The epigraph to "I Must Be Some Kind of Impossible" quotes Dawn Lundy Martin from her interview with Adam Fitzgerald, "On the Black Avant-Garde, Trigger Warnings, and Life in East Hampton," published on Lithub.com in December 2015.

The Biblical story of Daniel in the lion's den, to which "Gothic" alludes, can be found in chapter 6 of the Book of Daniel.

"Aubade: Apocalypse" (and, more liberally, "When What They Called Us Was Our Name") employs a device I've named CASH (consonantal anagrammatic slant homeoteleuton), in which each line, or each alternating line, ends in a word or phrase composed of the same set of recycled consonant sounds, with the purpose of insinuating a sonic motif or mood. The device takes some inspiration from Phillip B. Williams's poem "A Spray of Feathers, Black" (*Thief in the Interior*, 2016).

"Leaves of Grass" takes its title from the collection that Walt Whitman first published in 1855 and revised until his death.

"I Will Guide Thy Hand" is the final and decisive utterance of the character Black Phillip from the film *The Witch* (2015). The last line of the poem alludes to a ritual performed against enemies who manifest in dreams.

"Head of the Gorgon" was inspired in part by Audre Lorde's "Coal" and by poet Dan Beachy-Quick's lecture "The Monster in Me Is the Monster in You," delivered at Washington University in St. Louis in 2016.

Akasha, named in "When I Am Queen," is the title character of the vampire film *Queen of the Damned* (2002), the last film performance by Aaliyah, an icon of my childhood, who died the year before the film's release.

In "Ruthless," the phrase *I seem tame. (Touch me.)* is a riff on the final couplet of Sir Thomas Wyatt's "Whoso List to Hunt, I Know where is an Hind."

"When I Am Alien" is written from the perspective of the xenomorph monster at the center of my favorite film, *Alien* (1979). The monster is portrayed (in costume) by Bolaji Badejo, a six-foot-ten Nigerian artist and actor who died of sickle cell anemia in 1992.

"The Man in Black" shares its title with—and obliquely responds to—namely, the poem of the same title by Mark Strand (*Reasons for Moving,* 1968) and "Man in Black" by Sylvia Plath (*The Colossus and Other Poems,* 1960).

"When I Had the Haint" refers to the phenomenon known secularly as sleep paralysis, better known in the Black Southern mystic traditions of my home as simply "the haint."

"Open Season" is largely inspired by Shanequa Gay's series of paintings *FAIR GAME* as well as by the internet video "Buck fights back against a hunter! Go deer!" published on YouTube by SailorPluto247 in 2006. The poem ultimately alludes to Michael Brown Jr.'s being equated to a demon by his murderer.

"Say Wussho Price" takes its title from the chorus of Nas's "You Owe Me," sung by Ginuwine. The poem is inspired by Langston Hughes's "Warning," first published as "Roland Hayes Beaten [Georgia: 1942]" in *One-Way Ticket* (1949); and by chapter 5, verse 5 of the Gospel of Matthew, which reads, "Blessed are the meek, for they shall inherit the earth."

In "A Leadspray of Starlings," *brought to heel* paraphrases the words of United States politician Hillary Clinton, used in reference to young Black people in a speech Clinton gave in New Hampshire in 1996 as part of the campaign for her husband's second presidential term. (The *super-predatory* of "When I Am Alien" is borrowed from the same passage of this speech.)

"When I Was a Poet" samples William Cullen Bryant's "Thanatopsis," alludes to a line of Robert Frost's "Birches," and briefly borrows the quotation metrics used by Alice Notley in *The Descent of Alette* (Penguin Books, 1996). The poem borrows its first lines from the Book of Genesis, chapter 1, verse 2. The recording of "The Inch Worm" appears on the 1962 album *Coltrane*.

"If We Must Be the Dead" makes acrostic use of lines from Claude McKay's "If We Must Die" (*Harlem Shadows*, 1922) and borrows a phrase from Sterling Brown's "Salutamus" (*Southern Road*, 1932).

"When What They Called Us Was Our Name" samples the last line of section 3 of Timothy Donnelly's "Globus Hystericus," from *The Cloud Corporation* (Wave Books, 2010).

ACKNOWLEDGMENTS

I'd like to thank the editors and readers of the following publications in which many of these poems appear, sometimes in earlier versions: the Academy of American Poets' Poem-a-Day ("About the Bees"), *African American Review* ("The Undying"), *BOAAT* ("Every Cell in This Country Looks Like a Choice You Can Walk In and Out Of"), *Boston Review* ("The Personal Animal"), *Breakwater Review* ("Blackguard"), *Connotation Press* ("Gothic," "If We Must Be the Dead," "The Lorelei"), *Denver Quarterly* ("I Have Wasted My Life," "It Singing Over the Glass Field Comes," "The Man in Black"), *Guernica* ("The Hang-Up"), *Lambda Literary Poetry Spotlight* ("Minotaur"), *Nashville Review* ("Beneficence"), the *New Republic* ("This Is Really Happening"), the *Offing* ("A Leadspray of Starlings"), *Paperbag* ("The Whiteness of Achilles"), the Poetry Foundation's *PoetryNow* ("In a Daydream of Being the Big House Missus"), *Poetry* ("Of Someone Else Entirely," "I Will Guide Thy Hand," "When I Was a Poet"), the *Rumpus* ("Leaves of Grass"), the *Shade Journal* ("Head of the Gorgon"), the *Shallow Ends* ("When What They Called Us Was Our Name"), the *Southeast Review* ("Considering My Disallowance," "How Many Model Mutilations Make a Single Slave"), the *Tusculum Review* ("Aubade: Apocalypse"), *wildness* ("When I Had the Haint," "Ruthless"), *Winter Tangerine* ("Open Season").

Some of these poems were written or revised through generous gifts of funding, space, or time offered by the Regional Arts Commission of St. Louis, the Cave Canem summer retreat, the Center for African American Poetry and Poetics at the University of Pittsburgh, and Design Hotels' Further Troutbeck.

Abundant thanks to my editor, Erika Stevens, for her candor, diligent collaboration, and support.

I'm deeply grateful to the Conversation Literary Festival—and to the vision and generous spirit of Nabila Lovelace—for the opportunities to practice communal care, share resources, exchange knowledge, and further imagine Black space.

For their contributions to the creation or improvement of these poems in ways overt, subtle, and all substantial, I give thanks to Phillip B. Williams, Jayson P. Smith, Rickey Laurentiis, Jonah Mixon-Webster, francine j. harris, Dan Beachy-Quick, Carl Phillips, Mary Jo Bang, Marwa Helal, Hieu Minh Nguyen, Fatimah Asghar, Safia Elhillo, and Paul Tran. I'd also like to thank Shanequa Gay for her creative alliance, for the imaginative terrain of her visual work, and for the gift of that artwork featured on this cover, marshaling poems it has inspired.

FUNDER ACKNOWLEDGMENTS

Coffee House Press is an internationally renowned independent book publisher and arts nonprofit based in Minneapolis, MN; through its literary publications and *Books in Action* program, Coffee House acts as a catalyst and connector—between authors and readers, ideas and resources, creativity and community, inspiration and action.

Coffee House Press books are made possible through the generous support of grants and donations from corporations, state and federal grant programs, family foundations, and the many individuals who believe in the transformational power of literature. This activity is made possible by the voters of Minnesota through a Minnesota State Arts Board Operating Support grant, thanks to the legislative appropriation from the Arts and Cultural Heritage Fund. Coffee House also receives major operating support from the Amazon Literary Partnership, Jerome Foundation, McKnight Foundation, Target Foundation, and the National Endowment for the Arts (NEA). To find out more about how NEA grants impact individuals and communities, visit www.arts.gov.

Coffee House Press receives additional support from the Elmer L. & Eleanor J. Andersen Foundation; the David & Mary Anderson Family Foundation; Bookmobile; Dorsey & Whitney LLP; Foundation Technologies; Fredrikson & Byron, P.A.; the Fringe Foundation; Kenneth Koch Literary Estate; the Matching Grant Program Fund of the Minneapolis Foundation; Mr. Pancks' Fund in memory of Graham Kimpton; the Schwab Charitable Fund; Schwegman, Lundberg & Woessner, P.A.; the Silicon Valley Community Foundation; and the U.S. Bank Foundation.

THE PUBLISHER'S CIRCLE OF COFFEE HOUSE PRESS

Publisher's Circle members make significant contributions to Coffee House Press's annual giving campaign. Understanding that a strong financial base is necessary for the press to meet the challenges and opportunities that arise each year, this group plays a crucial part in the success of Coffee House's mission.

Recent Publisher's Circle members include many anonymous donors, Suzanne Allen, Patricia A. Beithon, the E. Thomas Binger & Rebecca Rand Fund of the Minneapolis Foundation, Andrew Brantingham, Robert & Gail Buuck, Dave & Kelli Cloutier, Louise Copeland, Jane Dalrymple-Hollo & Stephen Parlato, Mary Ebert & Paul Stembler, Kaywin Feldman & Jim Lutz, Chris Fischbach & Katie Dublinski, Sally French, Jocelyn Hale & Glenn Miller, the Rehael Fund-Roger Hale/ Nor Hall of the Minneapolis Foundation, Randy Hartten & Ron Lotz, Dylan Hicks & Nina Hale, William Hardacker, Randall Heath, Jeffrey Hom, Carl & Heidi Horsch, the Amy L. Hubbard & Geoffrey J. Kehoe Fund, Kenneth & Susan Kahn, Stephen & Isabel Keating, Julia Klein, the Kenneth Koch Literary Estate, Cinda Kornblum, Jennifer Kwon Dobbs & Stefan Liess, the Lambert Family Foundation, the Lenfestey Family Foundation, Joy Linsday Crow, Sarah Lutman & Rob Rudolph, the Carol & Aaron Mack Charitable Fund of the Minneapolis Foundation, George & Olga Mack, Joshua Mack & Ron Warren, Gillian McCain, Malcolm S. McDermid & Katie Windle, Mary & Malcolm McDermid, Sjur Midness & Briar Andresen, Daniel N. Smith III & Maureen Millea Smith, Peter Nelson & Jennifer Swenson, Enrique & Jennifer Olivarez, Alan Polsky, Marc Porter & James Hennessy, Robin Preble, Alexis Scott, Ruth Stricker Dayton, Jeffrey Sugerman & Sarah Schultz, Nan G. Swid, Kenneth Thorp in memory of Allan Kornblum & Rochelle Ratner, Patricia Tilton, Joanne Von Blon, Stu Wilson & Melissa Barker, Warren D. Woessner & Iris C. Freeman, and Margaret Wurtele.

For more information about the Publisher's Circle and other ways to support Coffee House Press books, authors, and activities, please visit www.coffeehousepress.org /pages/support or contact us at info@coffeehousepress.org.

LITERATURE
is not the same thing as
PUBLISHING

JUSTIN PHILLIP REED is the author of *Indecency* (Coffee House Press), winner of the 2018 National Book Award in Poetry and the Lambda Literary Award for Gay Poetry, and a finalist for the 2019 Kate Tufts Discovery Award. He was born and raised in South Carolina. *The Malevolent Volume* is his second collection of poems.

The Malevolent Volume was designed by
Bookmobile Design & Digital Publisher Services.
Text is set in Garamond Premier Pro.